A WO

Wordsworth Editions

First published in England 1993 by
Wordsworth Editions Ltd
Cumberland House
Crib Street
Ware
Hertfordshire SG12 9ET

ISBN 1 85326 990 5

Many illustrations in this
volume appear by courtesy
of the various breed societies
Right: a Turkish Van

Set in 8½/9pt Monophoto Univers
Text conversion and pagination by
August Filmsetting, St Helens

Printed in Italy by Amadeus s.p.a.

Contents

Longhair breeds

Shorthair breeds

Balinese

Identification: the Balinese is a long-haired Siamese and is a mutation of longhair kittens in a normal Siamese litter. It is never bred to another breed: only accepted in the four Siamese colours.

Head: long, tapering; wedge-shaped; of medium size, and well-proportioned to the body. The line of the wedge shape is carried on to the points of the ears. The muzzle is fine with a long nose; the skull is flat, with no bulge over the eyes.

Eyes: blue, almond-shaped; of medium size and slanting slightly towards the nose; they should not protrude or be recessed, and they should never be crossed

Ears: quite large, being wide at the base and fairly well feathered

Tail: long, quite thin and tapering to a point at the tip, and plumed

Body: medium size, longish, light and lithe yet well-muscled; legs are long and slender, in good proportion to the body, and provide very graceful movement. The hindlegs are slightly longer than the forelegs; the paws are small and oval. The neck is long and slender.

Coat: single coat, of long, fine and silky hair. It is important to note that there is none of the mane or collar which is so typical of other longhairs.

Colour: *seal point*, for which the body colour can range from pale fawn to cream, but of even

A Balinese seal point, showing the
beautifully wedge-shaped head

colour, lighter on the chest and belly. The points are a warm deep brown with the face being particularly well covered by the mask.

Chocolate point: should be an even ivory-colour coat with light chocolate markings

Blue point: a very white coat tinged with blue with dark blue markings, producing a very cold effect

Lilac point: a snow-white coat with pinkish-grey markings.

Origin: born in a litter of Siamese kittens in the USA in the 1950s, with long silky hair, these mutant kittens were the first of a new breed which was finally accepted by all Associations in 1970. The name was selected because of their graceful movement, not because they had any association with Bali, as they do not. A new name for the breed was also required because of the objection to 'longhaired Siamese' being recognised.

Personality: the Balinese is a happy cat, lively and extremely affectionate. Sociable and intelligent, a graceful acrobat, not keen on the outdoors; neither is it fussy with its diet. The texture of the coat makes it unlikely to tangle or to knot as much as that of other longhairs. Litters average three to four kittens; they mature sexually earlier than other longhairs and make intelligent parents.

8 *Balinese blue point*

Birman

Identification: a Persian coat quality and Siamese markings, on a dignified cat with a fascinating expression

Head: broad and round with full cheeks; strongly-boned with a strong mouth, rounded muzzle and straight nose with the nostrils set low

Eyes: roundish in shape; deep blue in colour; very slightly slanted with the outer corner tipping slightly forward

Ears: set wide apart; of medium size, being quite broad at the base

Tail: of medium length; well-proportioned; robust and well-feathered

Body: long, well-developed with thick-set legs of medium length; round, trim paws which are quite large, toes bound closely together

Coat: longish and silky, a thick ruff round the neck, well covered on the back and flanks and slightly wavy on the belly. The coat does not require as much grooming as other longhairs as the hair never becomes matted or tangled.

Colour: there are four colourpoints and all have characteristic pure white gloves on all four feet.

Seal point: pale cream body, even in colour and becoming lighter on the chest and belly; the points (mask, ears, tail and paws) are dark seal brown.

Blue point: bluish-white to pale ivory on the

Birman blue point; note the thick whiskers

body, shading to white on the chest and stomach, and grey-blue points. The blue point has an overall cold appearance.

Chocolate point: body is ivory free of shading, points are milk-chocolate coloured.

Lilac point: off-white body with pearl-grey points.

Origin: according to legend, the Sacred Cat of Burma, as it is known, existed centuries ago in the beautiful temples of the Khmer people in Asia, in order to pay homage to their gods. The cats in these temples were pure white, and it was believed that they were the embodiment of priests, who, after death, thus returned to the temples in the form of cats. The Temple of Lao Tsun housed a beautiful golden goddess, Tsun-Kyan-Kse, and by her side was always a white temple cat, Sinh. The temple was attacked, and the cat's master killed; when Sinh placed his feet upon his dead master, his white hairs turned golden as the moonlight was reflected off the golden goddess. The following morning, all the temple cats had changed. A pair of these cats was presented to the French in 1919.

Personality: sensitive and energetic; a good apartment cat; known to be good breeders

12   *Birman seal point*

Cymric

Identification: a longhaired Manx; the name derives from the Celtic name for Welsh, and is pronounced Kim'ric. (The Isle of Man, where the Manx originated, is located in the Irish Sea, roughly equidistant between Wales and Ireland.)

Head: almost round, being just slightly longer than it is wide, with prominent cheeks, round forehead and well-developed muzzle

Eyes: large and round, the outer corner slightly higher than the inner. The colour is determined by coat colour; most common is copper, but green, blue, hazel and odd eyes are also acceptable.

Ears: gradually tapered, from a wide base to a round tip

Tail: tailless

Body: solidly built, with well-developed muscles; broad chest; a short back forming an arch. The legs are heavily boned, with the forelegs set well apart and the hindlegs longer. Paws are tidy and round, the neck short and thick.

Coat: double-coated, with a thick undercoat. The outer coat is medium to long, with longer hair on the abdomen and breeches, plus a neck ruff.

Colour: all colours and combinations of colours

Origin: the Cymric appeared in a Manx litter in Canada, in about 1960, and selective breeding has produced a true breed

Personality: the Cymric is of varying temperament, but generally affectionate and very active

Himalayan/colourpoint longhair

Identification: a cobby, well-built cat like a longhaired Persian in Siamese colours

Head: round and massive, with a broad skull and a well-rounded face. The nose is short and broad; the cheeks are full, and the chin well-developed.

Eyes: large, round but not protruding; the eyes of pointed cats are usually a deep sapphire blue, and those of the solid-coloured cats, copper

Ears: set wide apart, the ears are small with rounded tips, slightly tilted forward, and not unduly opened at the base

Tail: this is carried lower than the back, straight without kinkiness, and is a full brush tail; shortish

Body: stockily-built, with short thick legs, and a short thick neck; chest deep; wide shoulders and rump, with a straight back. The paws are large, round and firm.

Coat: standing off from the body, the fine-textured coat is long, thick and glossy. There is a full neck ruff, which continues between the front legs to form a frill; long tufts on the ears and toes.

Colour: there are various recognised colours, but the body colour for all should be free of barring and only subtle shading is allowed. There should be a clear distinction between the body colour and the point colour. The mask should cover the whole face, including the whisker pads, and is connected to the ears by tracings. It should not extend over the top of the head.

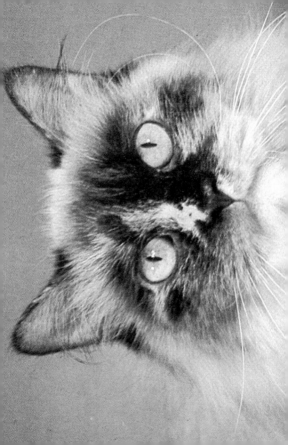

Seal point, thick cream coat with seal brown points (mask, ears, legs, feet and tail); *blue point,* cold, bluish-white coat with blue markings; *chocolate point,* ivory coat with milk-chocolate markings; *lilac point,* magnolia-white coat with frosty grey markings; *red point,* creamy-white coat with orange flame markings; *tortie point,* cream coat with tortoiseshell markings; *blue cream point,* blue-white coat with blue markings patched with cream. Lynx point, chocolate solid and lilac solid colours are also to be found.

Origin: first produced in the 1920s, the Himalayan is a hybrid cross between the Persian and the Siamese. The name derives from the Himalayan rabbit, because of similarities in colouration. In the UK, the breed was recognised in 1955 as the colourpoint longhair, and also with some USA registries; while in America generally it was recognised in 1957, following exports from the UK to help perfect the type. Since then, the popularity of the Himalayan has continued to increase steadily.

Personality: affectionate and good-natured, tends to be quiet but does love to play. They prefer a single owner and a big apartment. The coat needs daily attention to keep it free from matting. Litters are usually of only two or three, with the kittens remaining white until they develop their markings at about six months.

18 *Himalayan seal point*

Javanese

Identification: this is basically a Siamese cat with long fur and the colour range of the colour-point shorthair

Head: of medium size, in good proportion to the body. It forms a long wedge-shape, which starts at the nose and continues to the back of the skull. The skull itself is flat, the muzzle fine and also wedge-shaped.

Eyes: vivid blue, almond-shaped; they should not protrude or be recessed, but slant towards the nose. Eyes which cross are not appreciated.

Ears: very large, pointed and wide at the base

Tail: long, thin and tapering to a point with the hair on the tail well spread to form a plume

Body: a long, slender, finely-boned body of medium size. The muscles should be firm, the legs long and slender, and the hindlegs higher than the front. The paws are small, and oval in shape.

Coat: long, fine with a silky texture, no undercoat and no long collar, unlike the other longhaired breeds. The coat is basically identical to that of the Balinese.

Colour: whereas the Balinese has few accepted colours, the Javanese has the colour range of the colourpoint shorthair, which extends to sixteen different colourings and includes: *red point*, cream body with orange/red markings; *cream point*, cream body with buff markings; *lilac-*

cream point, ice-white body with grey/pink markings patched with cream.

Other colours are seal-lynx, chocolate-lynx, lilac-lynx, red lynx, seal-tortie, chocolate-tortie, blue-cream, seal tortie-lynx, chocolate tortie-lynx, blue-cream lynx, lilac-cream lynx and cream lynx. The lynx point has tabby markings on the points.

Origin: the Javanese is an expansion of the breeding of the Balinese, which was itself a mutant Siamese. The Balinese has only four accepted colours, which are seal point, blue point, chocolate point and lilac point, but the breeding programmes have expanded the range to be comparable with that of the colourpoint shorthair, which is itself a Siamese cat in other colours. Although the Balinese gained recognition in 1970, it was not until 1987 that the Javanese was accepted by the Cat Fanciers Association.

Personality: a reputation for being easy-going, but they do like to dominate their surroundings. The coat needs very little attention, and they are not fussy eaters; litters are usually of three or four kittens.

Kashmir

Identification: very Persian in type, and best described as a self-coloured Himalayan

Head: a broad, round head; short stub nose

Eyes: large, round and prominent

Ears: low-set, small; not very open at the base; tilted forward and rounded at the tips and tufted

Tail: in proportion to the body, not too long

Body: large, cobby body, set low and well-muscled. The back is level. The legs are short and thick; the forelegs straight, paws large, round and firm, with close-carried tufted toes.

Coat: dense woolly undercoat and long thick outer coat, which is off-standing and flowing, covering the entire body, including the shoulders. There is a large ruff continuing onto the chest and forelegs, and a full brush tail.

Colour: the most common colours are chocolate, which should be without shading and a soft brown in colour; or lilac, which should be a warm lavender colour with a pinkish tinge

Origin: born into litters of Himalayans/colourpoint longhairs, and bred into each other to create the pure coat; they are considered to be Persian/longhairs in the UK

Personality: calm, beautiful cats; very casual despite the cobby build, they prefer delicate handling and new-born kittens are fragile at birth and need close supervision. Coats need to be brushed on a daily basis.

Maine coon cat

Identification: a medium to large cat, graceful in appearance, with a shaggy coat which appears in a wide variety of colours, owing to its free roaming and breeding habits

Head: medium-sized in both width and length, being rather longer and with a definite squareness to the muzzle. The cheekbones are high, the chin firm and in line with the nose and upper lip; the nose is of medium length.

Eyes: large, set wide apart, with a slight slant towards the outer base of the ear. The colour should be yellowish or of a colour in harmony with the colour of the coat; only the white Maine coon cat has blue eyes.

Ears: large, well-tufted, wide at the base and tapering to appear somewhat pointed

Tail: long, wide at the base, tapering and thickly feathered

Body: a broad-chested, muscular cat with the overall body appearance being rectangular with a longish body and all parts in proportion. The legs are of moderate length; the paws are large, circular and well-tufted.

Coat: silky-textured fur falling smoothly along the cat's sides, heavy and shaggy, shorter on the shoulders and longer on the stomach. A full ruff is preferred.

Colour: the standard permits more than 20 col-

A beautiful and intelligent Maine coon tabby

ours, both solids and mixed, which break down into five classes: solids, tabbies, tabby and whites, partis and smokes or others. The solids are white, black, blue, red and cream. The tabby patterning includes mackerel and patched, in addition to classic. The class comprising smokes includes chinchilla and shaded silver.

Origin: Although not definitely confirmed, it is considered that the Maine coon cat was the result of crossings between New England local domestic cats and angoras. The angoras were the first long-coated cats to arrive in the USA, and the Maine coon was first recorded as early as 1861. However, it was not until 1953 that the Central Maine Coon Cat Club was established and the standard drawn up in 1967.

Personality: hardy and rugged, and despite their ancestry which has made them great mousers, they are home-loving and affectionate, very much the perfect pet. They should be groomed like an angora, with regular brushings to remove dead hairs. Litters are usually of only two or three and they do not mature fully until four years old.

A Maine coon in portrait, showing its
28 *angular body shape*

Nebelung

Identification: a graceful new breed, with similar characteristics to the Russian blue

Head: a wedge-shaped head with the skull flat at the top; a medium-sized nose

Eyes: round and wide-set, deep green in colour

Ears: large, with a nicely-rounded tip and a wide base; rather thin and full of feathering

Tail: long, broad at the base and tapering to the tip

Body: a long, fine-boned body with firm muscles; the legs are long, the paws small and slightly rounded

Coat: of medium length for a long-haired cat, but the tail is profusely plumed

Colour: clear, even blue with desired shades varying from place to place; for example, a lighter shade is preferred in the USA compared to that in the UK

Origin: an uncontrolled mating in 1982 produced a litter with two black female kittens and a male. One of these females was mated to a male believed to be a Russian blue, and this litter produced six kittens, all blue or black solid-coloured. One kitten from this litter and one from a subsequent litter from the same parents were bred in the USA to produce the Nebelung.

Personality: a pleasing, happy cat; affectionate and loving

Norwegian forest cat

Identification: a sturdy cat of medium size, in which the thickness of coat and physical soundness take precedence over colour

Head: a big, round, strong head with a wide forehead; a medium-long nose, and a firm chin that forms a line with the upper lip and nose

Eyes: bright, oval in shape; their colour depends on the coat colour. The eyes slant towards the outer base of the ears.

Ears: set high and wide apart

Tail: medium to longish in length, heavily coated and beautifully plumed

Body: muscular, broad-chested with well-boned strong legs and large round paws, with extraordinary claws that make the forest cat an excellent climber of trees and rocks

Coat: a heavy, thick coat which offers protection against the cold northern climate. There is also a thick, woolly undercoat. The hair is of medium length, shorter on the shoulders but they do have an extensive ruff. The thick coat is shed in early summer.

Colour: basically any colour is permitted; tabbies, solids, bi-colours and parti-colours

Origin: this is the single native breed of Scandinavia, and has survived in adverse weather conditions in the wild for centuries. Written about in Norwegian mythology and included in

32 *A tabby and white Norwegian forest cat*

Nordic fables, the breed was first recognised in 1930, and is still not recognised in the UK, where it is not numerous. Indeed, outside of Scandinavia the breed is very scarce.

Personality: alert and aware of its environment, the Norwegian forest cat is suspicious and intelligent; exactly what you would expect, considering its ancestry. They are fearless and enjoy human companionship, but need a large house with ample space to roam. An excellent hunter, quite able to provide its own food; occasional combing will suffice, and breeding is unproblematical.

Oriental longhair

Identification: a sleek, plush-coated cousin of the Oriental shorthair

Head: a long, tapering wedge shape with the line running unbroken straight from the tip of the nose to the top of the head. There is no indentation over the nose or lift for the eyes.

Eyes: moderately sized, almond-shaped; prominent but not protruding; the colour should be green but white cats may have blue eyes

Ears: very large and pointed; their lines continue the wedge shape on from the head

Tail: lengthy, thin at the base and tapering to a definite point and quite extensively plumed

Body: long and sleek; the legs are also long and slim, with the hindlegs longer than the forelegs

Coat: of medium length and thick

Colour: coat colours are various, with solids, tortoiseshell, smoke, tabby (all patterns) and shaded all acceptable. Smokes include blue, cameo, chestnut, ebony, fawn, cinnamon and parti-coloured.

Origin: an outbreeding of the Oriental shorthair, with the use of Persian crosses to obtain the required coat type and length

Personality: very sensitive, requiring time and attention. They should be groomed daily. Average litter size is three or four.

Persian/longhair

Identification: a rounded, solid appearance, with perfect proportions from head to tail and a healthy, flowing coat. In Europe and Britain, they are known simply as longhairs with each colour considered a separate breed with slightly different characteristics. In America they are all Persians, but of different colours.

Head: round and massive, with emphasis on the roundness; the nose is short and broad, with a definite stop, full cheeks and a broad, strong jaw. The chin should not protrude beyond the upper lip.

Eyes: full, large, round eyes; set far apart, they should be brilliant

Ears: set far apart; small with rounded tips; not unduly open at the base; they should be low on the head and tilted forward. The ears continue the roundness of the cat.

Tail: short, carried straight and at an angle lower than the back

Body: cobby, being short, deep in the chest and low on the legs. The shoulders are massive; the neck is short, strong and thick. The middle body section is well rounded and the rump is also wide across. The legs are short and strong, the forelegs straight; the paws are large, round and firm.

Coat: long and thick, standing off from the body. The hair is fine-textured and long all over the body, including the shoulders. An immense ruff,

which continues down between the front legs in a frill; ear and toe tufts are long and the tail full.

Colour: the recognised solid colours include blue-eyed white, copper-eyed white, odd-eyed white, red, cream, blue and black, in which the colour must be glossy black, uniform to the root, without patterns or light hairs or shading.

It is best to keep black Persian/longhairs out of the sun to avoid bleaching of the hair, which tends to turn towards brown. Breeding is difficult and kittens do not attain their true colour until about seven months of age. The eyes are big and bright, and deep orange or copper-coloured. The black Persian or black longhair is an exceptionally beautiful and affectionate cat.

Accepted colours also include chinchilla and shaded silver, blue smoke, black smoke and cameo smoke, shell cameo and shaded cameo, and in addition tortoiseshell. The tortoiseshell colours should be distinct and glossy, comprising black, red and cream. The eyes are orange or copper. Litters comprise mostly females, with the rare male being sterile. Female tortoiseshells must be mated with black, red or cream Persian/longhair males. The tortoiseshells are excellent mother cats, and more friendly and companionable than the majority of Persians. The tortoiseshell and white, which is closely related to the tortoiseshell, must be mated with bi-coloured

males.

Other colours recognised are calico, dilute calico, blue-cream, bi-colour, peke face red, peke face tabby, and classic patterned and mackerel patterned tabbies in blue, silver, red, cream, cameo and brown.

The brown tabby has a sand-brown base colour to the coat, with tawny tones and marbling formed by black bands that are 'streaked' in a way reminiscent of wild cats. The eyes are orange and stand out vividly from the dark coat. This is a difficult variety to produce because of the complicated patterns required by the standard. The brown tabby requires frequent brushing to remove knots. A gentle cat, that enjoys the reputation of being a good mouser.

Origin: descending from the long-coated Turkish angora cats

Personality: docile and quiet, it likes to sit around adorning the room, enjoys company, but can be aloof. Although they are not demanding, they do like attention, the females being more pushy. Good long sleepers, often in uncomfortable places. Daily brushing is essential, using a natural bristle brush, but this brushing should not be vigorous. Litters are generally two to three kittens, which need constant attention for about 16 weeks.

Tortoiseshell and white Persian/
longhair

Ragdoll

Identification: of good length, and quite solid; the ragdoll is a big cat with an imposing presence

Head: round, with prominent, well-developed cheeks; a medium-sized straight nose with a gentle stop. The head is broad between the eyes and ears; the forehead slopes down to a rounded, well-developed chin; it is flat in the centre between the ears.

Eyes: large and round; should not be crossed. The eyelid tilts slightly upwards at the outer edge. The eyes are coloured blue.

Ears: small to medium in length, and set high on the head, with a broad base and slightly rounded tip. The ears tilt slightly forward.

Tail: long and full

Body: heavy in the hind section, with large, loose muscles on the underside of the stomach. The legs are long and heavily boned, the hindlegs being longer than the forelegs. The neck is short and strong, the breastbone expanded.

Coat: thick and soft, medium to long; a very fluffy full ruff, and slight ear tufts. The coat does not matt.

Colour: split into three colour types; *bi-coloured*, usually a colour with white; *mitted* (cats with white mittens) and *mittenless* (cats without white mittens). Both the mitted and mittenless are colourpoints, which by colour, rather than by pattern, can be seal, chocolate, blue, cin-

44   *A frost bi-colour ragdoll portrait*

namon, fawn or lilac.

Origin: the ragdoll was originated in the 1960s, according to popular legend as the result of a Persian/longhair female which, following damage to the nervous system in an automobile accident, was unable to feel pain. This curious characteristic has supposedly been handed down to subsequent generations, together with the inability to recognise danger or feel afraid. Geneticists have doubts about this, suggesting that a more likely origin for the cats' docile temperament is the result of frequent breeding among domestic cats. Whatever the truth, the exact ancestral parentage is not documented, which makes the establishment of a standard difficult. The breed has, however, gained acceptance in the past ten years with some American registries.

Personality: the resultant ragdoll is a cat of infinite docility and gentleness, mild-mannered and affectionate. They seem to lack fear or any instinct of self-preservation. They are known for their limpness when being handled, like a ragdoll or bean bag; they literally go quite limp when picked up, and it is claimed that they may be picked up when asleep and not wake up as a result, even when shaken.

Longhair Scottish fold

Identification: a rugged cat, of medium size; well-rounded, with small folded ears

Head: round and broad, prominent cheeks, firm jaw and chin; well-rounded muzzle pads

Eyes: large, round and set wide apart; according to coat colour, the eyes can be copper, green, blue-green, hazel or golden

Ears: small, tightly folded forward and down

Tail: can vary between medium and long; the more tapering the better, and proportion should be in keeping with the body

Body: medium sized and well-rounded, being even from the hips up to the shoulder. The legs are shortish, with well-rounded toes.

Coat: flowing, soft and medium to long; ruffs and breeches a bonus; needs regular brushing

Colour: the colours are the same as for the Persian/longhair, with the exception of lilac and chocolate, and are blue, red, white, black, cream; chinchillas; smokes; and tabbies, which are divided into three patterns, described on pages 74–8: *classic, mackerel,* and *patched tabby;* brown, silver or blue patched in red and/or cream

Origin: longhair kittens had appeared in Scottish fold litters but the variant was established by crossing British shorthairs and other domestics.

Personality: determined and sociable

Brown mackerel tabby longhair
Scottish fold

Somali

Identification: agile, graceful and light-footed, a wild-looking longhaired Abyssinian

Head: a slightly rounded wedge, without any flatness; the cheeks, brow and profile lines are all bevelled, with a gentle rise from the bridge of the nose to the forehead. The muzzle is in keeping; the chin is full, being neither overshot nor undershot, and also has a rounded look.

Eyes: large and almond-shaped; preferred colours are deep gold or green, with a dark lid skin encircled by a light-coloured area. There is also a dark pencil line running from the upper eyelid towards the ear.

Ears: set well apart and to the rear of the head, the ears are large and moderately pointed. They are broad and cupped at the base and well tufted.

Tail: thick at the base and slightly tapering; well-covered, forming a full brush

Body: of medium length, with well-developed muscles. The rib cage is rounded and the back slightly arched. The legs are slender and sturdy, proportionate to the body in length; the feet are compact, and oval in shape.

Coat: double-coated; the outer coat should be of dense medium-length hair, soft and very fine. Ruffs and breeches are also preferred. The hair can be slightly shorter over the shoulders.

Colour: a soft blue-grey, ticked with slate blue; the undercoat is ivory-coloured, the tail is tipped

50 *A handsome ruddy Somali*

slate blue, the forelegs and underbody can vary from cream to beige. Ruddy, an orange-brown ticked with black with the inner legs and underbody solid ruddy in colour, and red, which is ticked with brown, the deeper the better, are also allowed. The full colour and ticking appear at about 18 months of age.

Origin: longhaired kittens began to appear in Abyssinian litters at the end of the 1960s, and although it is claimed that this first occurred in Canada, mutant longhairs were cropping up elsewhere. Supposedly the kittens were the result of crossings between the Abyssinian and a longhair, but the Somali is not a hybrid breed. Two Somalis bred together will breed true, producing Somali kittens, whereas a pair of shorthairs producing Somali kittens may not produce another Somali for several litters.

Personality: an entertaining and affectionate cat, the Somali is lively, curious and intelligent. They get on well with other breeds, being accommodating and patient. As they are a double-coated longhair breed, they require constant grooming, to keep the coat tangle-free and soft. They like the indoors, but need a large terrace or garden, especially in good weather conditions. Litters are usually of only two or three.

The beautiful Somali: note the full
tail

Turkish angora

Identification: a robust cat, graceful and with a more pointed face than the Persian, with the odd-eyed white being the most prized

Head: small to medium in size, wedge-shaped. Wide at the top, tapering towards the gently-rounded chin. The nose is of medium length and gently sloped without a break; the jaw is tapered.

Eyes: large and almond-shaped, slanting slightly towards the nose. The first angoras had blue or one blue and one orange eye. Those with blue eyes may be born deaf; different eye colours are now accepted, but are not advantageous.

Ears: wide at the base, the ears are long, pointed and tufted; they must be set high on the head

Tail: carried lower than the body, it should not drag and when the cat is mobile it should be carried over the back so that it almost reaches the skull. The tail is fully coated, long and tapering.

Body: medium-sized, fine-boned with a long torso; the rear higher than the shoulders. The legs are long, with the hindlegs being longer than the forelegs. The paws are small and round; the neck is delicate and graceful. The body of the male cat is larger.

Coat: single-coated, with fine silky hair; medium to long on the body, with a good ruff. The coat is wavier on the stomach and sheds a lot in summer.

Colour: originally accepted only if white; white

is still the preferred colour, but others which are now accepted varieties are black; blue; black smoke; blue smoke; silver tabby; red tabby; brown tabby; blue tabby, calico and bi-coloureds.

Origin: a natural breed, centuries old, originating in Ankara, Turkey, from which it derives its name (Angora was the ancient name for the city). On leaving Turkey, the cross-breeding that occurred in other countries led to the angora losing its identity at about the end of the nineteenth century. Fortunately the Ankara Zoo had been propagating a pure line of the breed, and it was from this line of white cats exported to Great Britain in the 1950s that the breed was re-established, as it was also in America in the 1970s. The Zoo still continues to breed pure white angoras, keeping to a strict breeding programme and meticulously recording the litters, that are bred once a year. The Turkish angora is recognised in America but not Britain, whereas the Turkish Van is recognised in Britain but not in America.

Personality: very alert and intelligent; friendly, loyal and long-lived; they are a pleasure to own. Kittens do not develop the angora coat until they are two years old.

A head shot of a white Turkish angora

Turkish Van

Identification: a delicate cat, born and bred near a lake; they are excellent swimmers, enjoying both a swim and a bath in tepid water

Head: wedge-shaped, tapering in a straight line towards the chin. The nose is long, with a coloured tip, and the pads are similarly tinted pink.

Eyes: large and almond-shaped, mostly amber but blues are acceptable; slanted outwards towards the ears

Ears: wide at the base, of good length and pointed at the tips. Pinkish in tone and well covered with hair.

Tail: long and tapering, carried lower than the body but not dragged. It is carried over the body when the cat is in motion.

Body: medium-sized long body, finely boned with the males slightly larger than the females. The rump is higher than the shoulders, the hindlegs longer than the forelegs. The legs are long, the paws small and round.

Coat: medium long, finely-textured and silky, but longer at the ruff, neck, belly and tail, which is profusely coated to make a full brush. The Turkish Van has only a single coat.

Colour: the ground colour should be a chalky white, although cream or off-white ground colours now exist. Markings over the eyes only are auburn. The tail is also auburn, in light and dark

The Turkish Van is a delicate, finely-boned cat with a dense coat

rings. It is important that the markings are not excessive.

Origin: taking their name from the Lake Van district of Turkey, where the two foundation cats were found in 1955. They are derived from the Turkish angora and were bred in Great Britain to establish coat pattern; the Turkish Van was recognised in Britain in 1969.

Personality: smart, playful individualists, enjoying human contact. Daily brushing is necessary to keep the coat in good condition. The Van cat is not a prolific breeder, producing about four kittens per litter, and needs encouragement. They tend to pick out one member of the family to favour. A good house cat, but they do like plenty of space; the more, the better.

Pink inside the ears, pink pads and nose are characteristics of the
Turkish Van

Abyssinian

Identification: an elegant little cat, with good muscle tone; not unlike a small puma, or the African wild cat, the Abyssinian is today one of the most sought-after of breeds

Head: moderately triangular in shape, it should not be sharp or rounded but gently contoured. The muzzle likewise should not be square or sharply-pointed, but is marked by a shallow indentation.

Eyes: set wide apart; they are large, bright and almond-shaped. Pencil markings under the eyes are characteristic. Eye colour can be green, hazel or yellow, and rimmed in black.

Ears: largish, and well-cupped; being moderately pointed, they have short tufts and are tipped

Tail: thick, long and tapering with a thick covering of fur

Body: slender and of medium length. The front legs are longer than the hindlegs, and are slim and finely-boned, with small compact oval feet with black pads. The neck is long with a swan-like arch.

Coat: double-coated, with an outer coat of short, fine-textured hair which is very thick and resilient to the touch, springing back when a finger is pushed across the coat against its lie. A characteristic of the Abyssinian is that each of the coat hairs has a light section at the root, and a

A ruddy Abyssinian, master of all it surveys

darker section at the tip, which is known as ticking. This creates an overall effect of an attractive fur with delicate shade variations.

Colour: ruddy, red, blue or cream. The coat should be ticked with distinct even-coloured bands of contrasting dark and light colours. The ruddy brown is ticked with various shades of black or dark brown; red coats are ticked with chocolate brown and a deep red undercoat, giving a warm effect throughout. Blue coats, which like the cream are not recognised in America, both colourations being very rare, are a soft blue-grey with slate blue tickings and an ivory undercoat. The cream is tinged with a pinkish buff, with the ticking a darker shade and the undercoat a light oatmeal.

Origin: the Abyssinian is believed to have descended from the ancient cats of Egypt, that were worshipped there more than four thousand years ago. The body type and facial structure and the entire presence of the Abyssinian certainly have a resemblance to the cats found in drawings and bronzes which date back to ancient Egypt. The theory is that the cat made its way from the Nile area over to Abyssinia (now known as Ethiopia). It was first brought to England in about 1868, at the time of the ending of the Abyssinian War, possibly by a returning soldier. In 1882 it gained recognition as a separate breed

64 *A head study of a red Abyssinian*

under the name of Abyssinian, but this was changed to ticked or British tick by the end of the century. The cats were exported to America and first shown in Boston in 1909; the first reported birth of an Abyssinian in America was in 1935, and it was named Addis Ababa. Today the Abyssinian is one of the most sought-after and loved cats.

Personality: highly intelligent, and easy to train. They love people and are very affectionate towards each other. They take a great interest in any events, and have a musical voice, but do not take kindly to confinement indoors, preferring a small garden. They love to climb trees. Diets have to be carefully controlled as they have a healthy appetite with a special preference for meat. To keep the coat soft and shiny, it should be brushed and rubbed with a cloth every day. Females are not prolific breeders and in addition frequently experience difficult pregnancies. For this reason, the female must be carefully watched during the pregnancy to guard against dangerous falls – they remain very active and adventurous during the pregnancy – and fractures occur easily. Litters are usually of three to four kittens, which are born with dark marks on their coats; these disappear after a period of about four months, the kittens being slow to develop.

66 *A red Abyssinian*

American bobtail

Identification: an elegant yet stockily-built cat, of which there are still relatively few; the bobtail is natural

Head: broad, with strong jaws and a nearly straight nose, with a gentle break being acceptable

Eyes: large, slightly rounded; in the colourpoint the eyes are blue, while the eyes of all others correspond to the coat colour

Ears: set well down, medium to large in size and wide at the base

Tail: it does exist and should be between 25-100mm (1-4in) and end in a point or knot. A full tail or docked tail is not acceptable.

Body: longer than it is tall, appearing to be quite low to the ground. The males are more muscular than females, with broader shoulders. The legs are short and well boned.

Coat: ranges between medium/short and medium/long; it does not mat

Colour: all colours and all patterns

Origin: an original cross between a seal point Siamese and a short-tailed tabby male produced offspring which were also crossed with Birman and Himalayan until eventually the breed was stabilised and the American bobtail established.

Personality: sweet and intelligent, they are very loyal. A quick brush is all that the non-matting coat requires.

American curl

Identification: a medium-sized cat, with distinctive small curled ears

Head: medium in size, being longer than it is wide; the muzzle is neither pointed nor square, but gently contoured; the muzzle break should not be pinched. The chin should be firm.

Eyes: medium to large; walnut-shaped; colour dependent on coat

Ears: characteristic of the breed, being wide at the base and rounded at the tip, they curl back attractively in a smooth arc. The tufting inside the ear is quite long.

Tail: wide at the base and tapering; well plumed

Body: the length of the body should be one and one-half times the shoulder height; a well-boned but not cobby cat. The legs are of medium length with medium-sized round paws.

Coat: of medium length, lying flat to the body and silky in texture; there should not be a ruff

Colour: any colour

Origin: derived from a black longhair stray that was found in Lakewood, California. The stray was a mutant with the gracefully curled ears. Carefully bred, the American curl has been quickly recognised as a unique breed.

Personality: charming and curious, the curl is a good patient mouser. When breeding, only one parent need be a curl.

American shorthair

Identification: a powerful-looking cat, pleasant to the eye like a well-trained athlete

Head: large, with a pleasant full-cheeked face which is slightly longer than its width. The nose is medium-sized, of uniform width and with a gentle curve. The muzzle is square, the chin well-developed and firm; substantial whiskers.

Eyes: set wide apart; round and bright; brilliant gold, copper, green, blue-green or hazel.

Ears: set wide apart and erect. They are medium in size, slightly rounded at the tip and should not be too open at the base.

Tail: medium length, in keeping with the body; heavy at the base, tapers to a blunt end

Body: medium to large, with heavy shoulders and well-developed chest. The neck is muscular and of medium length, the legs are medium in length, well-muscled with firm bones. The paws are firm, with solid pads which are full and round.

Coat: short, thick with an even hard texture, quite able to withstand weather, thorns or scratches. In winter, it becomes thicker.

Colour: the colour range is full and varied: *red*, deep, rich, brilliant red without colour variation or ticking; one of the more difficult colours to achieve; gold eyes. *White*, pure, glistening white with either gold eyes, blue or odd-eyed (one gold and one blue); *black*, coal black, solid on the hairs, without signs of smoke or rustiness;

gold eyes. *Blue,* a solid, even grey, lighter shades being preferred, gold eyes; *cream,* the colour must be even, with lighter shades of the buff cream preferred; gold eyes. *Chinchilla,* pure white on the undercoat, chin, ear tufts, stomach and chest, with the longer hairs on the back, flanks, head and tail tipped with black to produce a shimmering silver effect. Eye rims, lips and nose are outlined in black; the nose is brick red, paw pads black, eyes green or blue-green. *Shaded silver,* basically as the chinchilla, but the black tipping is much stronger; *shell cameo* or *red chinchilla,* as the chinchilla, but with red replacing the black; this includes the eye rims, nose and paw pads; gold eyes. *Shaded cameo* or *red shaded,* as the shaded silver, but with a deep red replacing the dark black tipping; gold eyes. *Black smoke,* black with a white undercoat, only apparent when the cat moves, gold eyes; *blue smoke,* grey with a white undercoat, gold eyes; *cameo smoke,* red with a white undercoat and gold eyes.

The tabby patterns for which the breed is renowned are classified in three groups. The *classic tabby* pattern has clearly-defined broad dense markings, with legs evenly barred with bracelets which stack high to meet the body markings. The tail is evenly ringed, and there are several unbroken necklaces on the neck and

74 *A red mackerel tabby*

upper chest. The letter M is formed on the forehead by frown marks. Lines over the back of the head extend to the shoulder markings which form the shape of a butterfly, with both the upper and lower wings distinctly outlined. The back markings consist of a line running down the spine to the tail, with a parallel stripe on each side, these three stripes separated by stripes of the ground colour. The side markings should be the same on both sides and there should be a row of 'buttons' on the chest and stomach.

The *mackerel tabby* pattern is also dense and clearly-defined, but formed by narrow pencillings. The legs are evenly barred with bracelets, the tail is barred, and the neck and chest have several chain-like necklaces. The M appears on the forehead; unbroken lines run back from the eyes and others run down from the head to meet the shoulders. The lines running down the spine form a narrow saddle, and narrow pencillings run around the body. *Silver tabby*, pale silver with black markings, black paw pads, and red nose; green or hazel eyes. *Red tabby*, red, with darker red markings; the lips, chin, nose and paw pads are red, eyes gold; *brown tabby*, coppery brown, with black markings; the nose is red, eyes gold. *Blue tabby*, bluish-ivory, with dark grey markings, gold eyes; *cream tabby*, a light cream colour with darker

76   A red classic tabby

markings; the nose and paw pads are pink, eyes gold. *Cameo tabby*, off-white, with red markings; the nose and paw pads are rose-coloured, eyes gold.

The *patched tabby* or *tortie* comprises a brown, blue or silver tabby with red and/or cream patches: *brown patched tabby*, coppery brown with classic or mackerel tabby black markings, and patches of red and/or cream; gold eyes. *Blue patched tabby*, bluish-ivory, with classic or mackerel tabby dark grey markings and patches of cream; gold eyes. *Silver patched tabby*, pale silver, with classic or mackerel tabby black markings and patches of red and/or cream; gold or hazel eyes. *Tortoiseshell*, black, with patches of red and cream, gold eyes; *calico*, white, with patches of black and red, gold eyes; *dilute calico*, white, with patches of blue and cream, gold eyes; *blue cream*, grey with patches of cream, gold eyes; *bi-colour*, white, with patches of black, blue, red, or cream; gold eyes.

Origin: European shorthairs emigrated to America with their masters and became Americans

Personality: intelligent, affectionate, homeloving, an excellent climber, and jumper and mouser; breeding is not a problem, and the usual litter size is four to six.

American wirehair

Identification: a unique breed, distinguished from all others by a change in the guard hairs of the coat, which instead of being smooth and tapering are crimped along the shaft and hooked at the end

Head: round and well-proportioned, with prominent cheeks. A well-developed muzzle and chin, which is also firm. There is a slight whisker break. The nose in profile shows a gentle concave curve.

Eyes: large, round, bright and clear, set well apart. The eye colour varies, but in solid whites odd eyes must be blue and gold; normal eye colours are gold, green, blue-green or hazel.

Ears: set wide apart, medium in size

Tail: in proportion to the body, tapering from a well-rounded rump to a well-rounded tip

Body: medium to large, with a level back. The shoulders and hips are the same width. The torso is well rounded. The legs are medium in length and bone and are well-muscled, with compact oval paws. Males are larger than females.

Coat: of medium length, tight and springy. The individual hairs are crimped (hooked or bent); the overall wiry appearance takes preference over individual hair.

Colour: like the American shorthair. The solid colours include white, black, blue, red, and

Head study of an American wirehair red and white bi-colour

cream; silver and red chinchillas; black, blue and red smokes, and tabbies but not patched tabbies. There are also bi-colours.

Origin: the American wirehair is a genetic mutation and the most recent to occur among domestic cats in America, which is the only country in which it has appeared so far. The mutation originated in a male kitten born into a litter of farm cats in 1966, in New York. At maturity this was bred with another cat from the same litter; they produced four kittens, two of which were wirehaired, and eventually through a series of selective breedings the American wirehair was established as a breed.

Personality: a robust, sweet-tempered cat, with many of the attributes of its American shorthair ancestry, being energetic and playful. Grooming should be carefully carried out and not too extensive, as the hair must remain wiry not wavy, and the coat is anyway resistant and virtually self-maintaining. Litters are usually of four kittens, and the wirehair is an excellent parent; like their shorthair cousins, they also like open spaces to roam in.

82 *An American wirehair brown tabby*

Bengal

Identification: a beautifully elegant large cat

Head: small in comparison to its body, the head is a broad modified wedge with rounded contours, longer than it is wide. The nose bridge extends beyond the level of the eyes. The nose is large and wide, the muzzle full and broad; the whisker pads are large, with high cheekbones.

Eyes: large and set wide apart

Ears: short, wide at the base; rounded tips

Tail: thick, medium in length, tapered at the end with a rounded tip

Body: large and long; well-muscled and heavy-boned. The legs are medium to long, and the hindlegs are longer than the forelegs and well muscled; the paws are large and round.

Coat: shortish in length, thick and luxurious with a lovely warm soft texture

Colour: there are three colour groups; leopard, snow leopard and marble leopard. The spots are random or pattered horizontally and may be black, brown, tan, chocolate (in various shades) or cinnamon (also in various shades).

Origin: developed by crossing the Asian leopard cat initially with Egyptian maus in the 1960s, in an attempt to preserve in one form or another the exquisite wild cat from extinction.

Personality: outgoing and affectionate, they need gentle daily grooming; careful study of their character will help in our understanding of them

Bombay

Identification: beautifully sleek, solid black cats which are slowly gaining in popularity

Head: pleasantly rounded, without flat planes, with a full face and short, well-developed muzzle and a visible nose break. The skull is rounded at the top between the ears; the nose is black.

Eyes: set wide apart, round, and ranging from yellow to deep copper in colour

Ears: set wide apart, medium in size, broad at the base with slightly rounded tips and tilted slightly forward

Tail: straight and of medium length

Body: muscular and of medium size, rather bulky in the males, which are appreciably heavier and larger than the females

Coat: fine and short, close-lying with a satin-like texture

Colour: black right down to the hair roots, with a shimmering lustre, uniform with no shading

Origin: the Bombay was developed in America from crossings between the Burmese and a black American shorthair. Appearing in the early 1970s, it was named after the city of Bombay because of its resemblance to the Indian black leopard.

Personality: delightfully even-tempered, the Bombay has been developed as the perfect house cat, not requiring the outdoors, sociable and decorative

British shorthair

Identification: a powerfully-bodied cat, of natural origins; it has a hint of Persian, but is distinctive and unlike the American shorthair

Head: broad, with well-rounded contours; well-developed cheeks and a short, broad nose and good muzzle with a recognisable stop beyond the whisker pad; chin firm, well developed.

Eyes: round, large and alert. The colour varies according to the coat colour and can be brilliant gold, copper, green, blue-green or hazel. Whites may have blue, orange or one eye sapphire-blue and the other orange, copper or golden.

Ears: set wide apart, with the base of the inner ear perpendicular to the outer corner of the eye; a broad base, round tip and medium size

Tail: in proportion to the body, thick at the base and slightly tapered

Body: medium to large, with broad, flat shoulders and hips the same width as the shoulders. The chest is broad and rounded, the neck short and strong; the legs are strong, with feet and toes well rounded.

Coat: a single coat; short, well-bodied and firm to the touch; dense, without being woolly

Colour: the British shorthair occurs in almost every possible colour, officially in no less than 17, and includes the very popular tabby, which is often regarded as a separate breed because of its unique markings. *White* cats may be blue-eyed

or orange-eyed or odd-eyed (one blue and one orange eye); the colour should be a pure white with no yellowing. *Black* cats must also be of pure colour; the eyes are orange, and there must be no green rims around the eyes, which is a serious fault. *The British blue* is often considered a separate breed. The coat should be evenly shaded deep grey (blue by cat fancy definition). It is important that both paw pads and nose leather are also blue; eyes are copper or orange. Other solid colours include lilac, chocolate, red and cream, which is a difficult colour to achieve without markings or white; the eyes are orange.

Tabby markings are divided into three patterns, all of which must have the letter M formed on the forehead by frown marks. *Classic tabby* patterning has contrasting pattern and ground colours. The legs and tail are ringed, the chest has unbroken lines running across, a butterfly shape on the shoulders, three dark spinal strips running from neck to tail and spirals on the sides. On the muzzle there are thin stripes running out from the nose. *Mackerel tabby* pattern replaces the butterfly shape with a series of narrow lines which run vertically down from the spine. Markings are altogether thinner and more pencil-like than the thicker markings of the classic pattern, and produce a more tiger-like appearance. Popular colours are silver tabby with green or hazel eyes and

red or black nose, and brown tabby with orange, hazel or yellow eyes. *Patched tabby* is the third tabby pattern, which is an established brown, silver or blue with patches of red and/or cream.

A *spotted* coat is a classic tabby pattern with spots throughout the design. The colours are silver or brown with black spots or red with deeper red spots. *Tortoiseshell* is black, with well-defined patches of cream and red; paw pads and nose may be either pink or black and the eyes copper or orange. The colours should be equally balanced and there should be no trace of tabby or white. *Tortoiseshell and white* has patches of black, cream and red on a white ground coat, but white should always be the smallest of the colours in area; eyes copper or orange. *Bi-colour* is any solid colour with white; copper or orange eyes. *Smoke:* black or blue cats, with a pale silver undercoat and no trace of white or tabby, yellow or orange eyes. *British tipped* or *shorthair colourpoint* comprises a white undercoat tipped, in any of the solid colours mentioned above, on the back, flanks, head, ears and tail; the eye colour depends on the colour of the tipping.

Origin: the British shorthair is both ancient and natural, having populated the towns of England for centuries. First shown in exhibition at the end of the nineteenth century, the standard was created by one Harrison Weir, who established

the British shorthair as the most successful show cat of the time. It was usurped by the imported Persian/longhair at the beginning of the twentieth century, but gained popularity again in the 1930s, only for World War II to intervene.

In an effort to restore the breed after the war, Persian/longhairs were introduced but because the crosses did not produce cats that met registration qualifications, they have been successfully bred out again. A supplementary register was used; the cats produced from longhair and shorthair crosses were registered in this until three generations of British shorthair to British shorthair had again purified the breed.

Today British shorthairs are only bred to British shorthairs, and the cat we see today, with just a subtle hint of Persian, dates from the 1950s.

Personality: strong, healthy and intelligent; charming and loving to both humans and other animals. Not easily upset, they are active, inquisitive and playful. They are self-cleaning, self-grooming; not a cat to be given a bath. Litter sizes are an average of three to four.

A cream mackerel tabby British
shorthair

Burmese

Identification: a medium-sized cat, with good bone structure, good muscular development, expressive eyes and a sweet face

Head: nicely rounded, with a full face and breadth between the ears. The face tapers to a short, well-developed muzzle. There is also a visible stop and the chin is rounded and firm.

Eyes: set wide apart, the eyes are big, round and golden – the deeper, the better

Ears: set well apart, medium-sized; broad-based, slightly rounded tips and tilted slightly forward

Tail: medium length, straight, tapers at the tip

Body: of medium size, compact and muscular, a rounded chest and long neck with a level back from shoulder to tail. In Britain the standard calls for a longer appearance than in America; the legs are long and slender, with well-shaped oval feet.

Coat: fine, glossy, short and lying close to the body, with a satin-like texture; the glossiness is a feature of the breed

Colour: the original colour of the Burmese was brown; sable brown in the USA, and seal brown in the UK. Acceptance of different colourations also differs as follows.

In the UK, additional colours are red, cream, blue, lilac, chocolate brown, tortie, chocolate tortie and lilac tortie, while in the USA the Bur-

mese now incorporates what was once a separate breed, the Malayan. This occurred in three colours: *champagne*, a warm honey-beige shading towards a light golden tan; *blue*, a medium tone with warm fawn undertones, and *platinum:* a silvery grey with pale fawn undertones.

Origin: according to legend, the breed originated in Burmese monasteries, where it was venerated as divine. A book of poems from the Ayudhya period (1350-1767) of Thailand describes the Burmese cat in addition to the Siamese and the Korat. The Burmese of today can be traced back to a female 'Burmese' with a brown coat imported into the USA from Rangoon, named Wong Mau. She was mated to a Siamese, and following years of careful selection and recrossings, the breed gained recognition in 1936.

Personality: affectionate, intelligent, loving and inquisitive; the Burmese is a superb cat in possession of a fine loud voice. They like plenty of attention, even from strangers, and are ideal for both the country house and city apartment, especially one with a terrace. A good rubdown with a grooming glove is appreciated and helps to keep the coat clean. Litters average five; the female goes into her first heat at seven months and the Burmese is long-lived.

98 *American sable, the traditional colour of the Burmese*

California spangled

Identification: a beautiful, rare and costly breed, created to ensure the continuation of the spotted coats that adorn the threatened wild cats

Head: medium in both length and width, with a slightly domed forehead, the muzzle is full with a slight stop between the forehead and nose; both the chin and the jaw are strong

Eyes: medium to large in size, almond-shaped and open; the colour is according to coat colour

Ears: of medium size; equal in height to their width at the base. Their tips are rounded.

Tail: full throughout, with a blunt black tip

Body: a medium-sized body, long and lean, carried low and evenly. The frame is muscular, the legs strong with powerful thighs and medium-sized feet.

Coat: short and velvety, close-lying on the back, sides, neck and face, with longer hair on the tail and underbelly

Colour: a spotted cat; the colours include silver, charcoal, gold, red, brown and black. The tops of the forelegs are marked with dark bars.

Origin: the result of a controlled programme to ensure the future of some wild cats from extinction. The breeding involved a feral Egyptian cat, a tropical house cat from South-East Asia and no fewer than six common breeds.

Personality: athletically active, the California spangled has a high degree of intelligence

Chartreux

Identification: a solid, muscular cat; a natural breed originating in France, with a woolly coat, slightly longer than that of the domestic shorthair
Head: large and broad but not round. The nose is short and straight; a slight stop is acceptable. The muzzle is narrow compared to the head size, but not pointed. The cheeks are well-developed, the jaws powerful with almost black lips.
Eyes: large, round and expressive; pale gold to orange in colour
Ears: set high on the head, always erect, small to medium in size with slightly rounded tips. Inside furnishings cover one half of the ear, with a very fine coat on the outer ear.
Tail: heavier at the base, tapering slightly to the tip and carried over the back
Body: large, well-proportioned and robust, with a well-developed chest and muscular shoulders. The neck is short, strong and heavy-set; legs are muscular and the gait noble. The paws are round and medium in size, the pads rose-taupe in colour. Males are somewhat bigger and heavier than the females.
Coat: dense and soft, longer than that of the domestic shorthair. The female's coat may be silkier and thinner than the male's, which has a slightly woolly texture.
Colour: all shades of blue-grey are permitted, but the lighter the more highly-prized. The skin is

completely blue.

Origin: believed to be a natural breed originating in France, where it has been part of the scene for centuries. The name is said to have been taken from the order of Carthusian monks who were supposed to have brought the cat from the Cape of Good Hope in the seventeenth century to their monastery *le grand Chartreux*. Certainly cats lived with monks throughout Europe, but it is more likely that the name originated from a French-imported Spanish wool known as *pile de Chartreux*, which would be an apt description of a cat with a thick woolly coat. In France breeding began about 1928, and cats first appeared in shows under the name Chartreux in 1931 in Paris. After World War II, the breed was re-established with the use of French blue cats from the countryside, as breeding out British shorthairs and Persians had led to a loss of type. Thus there are now three types of blue cats to be found in France.

Personality: a gentle, affectionate cat, very independent and softly-spoken.; good mousers, enjoying a lot of space. A regular brushing will suffice for this hardy and uncomplaining individual.

Colourpoint shorthair

Identification: a fine-boned, medium-sized cat, dainty and svelte with long tapering legs

Head: medium in size, it forms a long tapering wedge beginning at the nose and flaring to the tips of the ears. The wedge gives a triangular appearance and there is no break at the whiskers. The skull is flat with no bulges in the face and no dip in the nose, which is long, slender and straight; the muzzle is fine and wedge-shaped.

Eyes: the width between the eyes should be no more than that of one eye; medium-sized, almond-shaped and normally a dark vivid blue.

Ears: large and pointed, wide at the base; they continue the line of the wedge

Tail: long and thin, it tapers to a fine point

Body: the stomach is tightly muscled and the same in width at the shoulders and at the hips. The legs are long and slim, the hindlegs longer than the forelegs; feet are small and oval, with five toes to the fore and four to the hind feet.

Coat: short, close-lying, fine-textured, glossy

Colour: the body coat is evenly coloured; delicate shading is allowed but clear colour preferred. The contrast between body colour and points is of great importance to colour quality. The coat generally darkens with age. The following colours are acceptable; the points are the face mask, ears, legs, feet and tail. *Red point,* white coat with dark red points; *cream point,* white

coat with apricot points; *seal-lynx point*, fawn coat with tabby points in light and dark brown; *chocolate-lynx point*, ivory coat with tabby points in light and dark brown; *blue-lynx point*, bluish-white coat with tabby points in contrasting shades of grey; *lilac-lynx point*, white coat with tabby points in contrasting shades of pinkish-grey; *red-lynx point*, white coat with tabby points in contrasting shades of red; *seal-tortie point*, fawn coat with brown points mottled with red and cream; *chocolate-cream point*, ivory coat with brown points mottled with cream; *blue-cream point*, bluish-white coat with dark grey points mottled with cream; *lilac-cream point*, white coat with pinkish-grey points mottled with cream.

Origin: the original Siamese had a fawn coat colour with seal brown points. It was later bred with chocolate, lilac and blue points, which were all accepted in both the UK and USA. The Siamese was then crossed with Abyssinians and other shorthairs to extend the range of available points. In America they are classed separately as colourpoint shorthairs because of the introduction of non-Siamese genes; but they are registered as Siamese in the UK.

Personality: active and inquisitive like the Siamese, a complex and sensitive cat

Cornish rex

Identification: a fine-boned delicate cat, very agile and fast-moving, with a wavy coat

Head: a small narrow head, about one-third again as long as it is wide. There is a definite whisker break. The muzzle narrows slightly to a rounded end. The nose is roman, one-third of the length of the head; the cheeks are lean and muscular, the chin strong and well-developed.

Eyes: medium in size, oval in shape and slanted slightly upwards; the eyes are set a full eye's width apart. Colour is determined by coat colour, but is most commonly gold; green, hazel, blue, blue-green and odd-eyed also appear.

Ears: placed high on the head, and held erect; the ears are large, wide at the base and come to a modified point at the top

Tail: long and flexible, the tail is slender and tapering to the end

Body: small to medium, with a long slender torso. The back is arched, with the lower line of the body following an upward curve. The shoulders are well-knit and the rump rounded and well-muscled. The legs are straight, long and slender, with well-muscled hips; paws are dainty and slightly oval in shape.

Coat: short and very soft, dense and silky; the coat is completely free of guard hairs, close-lying with the fur on the underside of the chin and on the breast and abdomen short and wavy

Colour: the colour range is wide; solid colours include blue-eyed, copper-eyed, and odd-eyed white; chinchilla; shaded silver; blue and black smokes; tabbies of various patterns and colours; tortoiseshells; calicos including dilute calico; blue-cream and bi-colour plus other rex colours, i.e. any other colour or pattern with the exception of those showing hybridisation resulting in the colours chocolate, lavender, the Himalayan pattern or these combinations with white

Origin: the rex has appeared as a spontaneous mutation on several occasions in several places. It reduces guard hairs and creates a wavy coat. In Cornwall, England, in 1950 when a curly-coated kitten was born into an otherwise normal litter of a tortie and white domestic shorthair mother and a ginger-coloured male, it was later bred back to its mother and produced more curly-coated kittens. Other rex mutations have occurred and have given us the German rex, the Oregon rex and the Devon rex, featured on page 114. These are separate varieties, and the Cornish is the most sparsely-coated rex.

Personality: a quiet and honest cat, inquisitive and affectionate; a creature of habit, well-suited to apartment life. Only pairs of the same breed and variety must be coupled, although in America the Cornish rex is crossed to the German rex, retaining the title of Cornish rex.

112 *A blue-eyed white*

Devon rex

Identification: even the whiskers are curly

Head: a medium-length wedge; overall very similar to the Cornish rex, but with fuller cheeks, shorter nose and a more pronounced stop

Eyes: large, oval and slanted towards the outer edges of the ears

Ears: larger and set wider apart than on the Cornish rex

Tail: very long, tapering to the tip; fine short fur

Body: a muscular body, long and lean and with a broad chest. The hindlegs are longer than the front legs; the paws are neat and oval.

Coat: must be dense overall, but most particularly on the back, sides, legs, tail, ears and face; the forehead need not be thickly covered. It must have a full-bodied texture, soft and fine; it is short and at its shortest on the upper anatomy of the cat and the chest; it must be wavy, producing a rippling effect; there are guard hairs.

Colour: a wide variety of colours; most popular are the solid colours, mainly with gold eyes. There also exists a Si-rex (Siamese rex) which displays white Siamese colourations.

Origin: established just ten years after the Cornish rex. When bred to the Cornish rex, they were unable to produce curly-coated kittens.

Personality: agile, intelligent and independent; they are good mothers, the usual litter varying between three and six

114   *A Devon rex white*

Egyptian mau

Identification: a graceful, cobby cat of medium size with a unique coat, spotted like no other

Head: a modified, slightly rounded wedge, lacking flat planes and with a gentle contour to the cheeks and the brow; the muzzle is not pointed.

Eyes: large, almond-shaped, slanted slightly upward towards the ears. The colour is light green, but an amber cast is also acceptable.

Ears: large and moderately pointed; broad at the base and erect, with ample space between them. The hair on the ears is short and close-lying; the inner ear is shell-pink, almost transparent.

Tail: medium-long; thick at the base; tapers slightly to the dark tip; heavily banded.

Body: medium length; hindlegs longer than the front; small dainty paws

Coat: fine, dense and silky-textured; resilient to the touch, medium length, long enough to accommodate two or more bands of ticking

Colour: there should be a good contrast between the pale ground colour and the deeper markings. The forehead bears the characteristic 'M', together with frown marks which form lines between the ears, continuing down the back of the neck and then breaking into elongated spots along the spine, which run together at the rear haunches to form a dorsal stripe continuing to the tail tip. The markings on the face and head are finer, the first starting at the outer corner of the

eye and continuing along the contour of the cheek; the second starts at the centre of the cheek and curves upwards; they almost meet below the base of the ear. The chest is ringed with one or more necklaces which should be broken in the centre. The markings across the shoulders are more than spots but not quite stripes. The upper part of the front legs is heavily barred. Markings on the body are a random mix of spots in different shapes and sizes, with the spots on the haunches and upper hindlegs almost running into stripes. The underside of the body should have dark buttons. There are three colours: *silver,* with charcoal markings; *bronze,* with dark brown markings, and *smoke,* grey and silver with black markings.

Origin: probably does go back to ancient Egypt, but the modern Egyptian mau dates from 1953, when a female Egyptian was imported into Italy by Princess Natalie Troubetskoye, and mated to another Egyptian. They produced two kittens, and the male kitten was later bred back to the mother and the breed began.

Personality: wise and docile, yet a good hunter. They like a lot of attention and have a really feline nature but a bird-like voice; well suited to small apartments, and excellent parents.

European shorthair

Identification: a medium to large cat

Head: a round, large head marked by well-developed cheeks. The nose is short, straight and of medium size; the chin firm, and strong. The muzzle is well-developed and there is a definite stop beyond the whisker pads.

Eyes: large and round, and according to coat colour may be gold, copper, green or blue-green or hazel. The white may have blue, orange or odd eyes, with one sapphire blue, the other orange, copper or golden.

Ears: set wide apart; medium size, rounded at the tips, and broad at the base

Tail: in proportion to the body; of medium length, thick at the base, and tapering

Body: sturdily built with a level back and broad deep chest; the legs are powerful and short to medium in length. The paws are round and firm.

Coat: a well-bodied single coat, short and resilient but never woolly although sometimes bristly

Colour: most colours are considered as separate breeds, an acknowledgment of the different genes that were required to create them. *European black:* a very widespread breed, with a beautiful glossy black coat and amazing eyes of yellow, orange or copper. Regarded as a fearless combatant. Not accepted are green eyes, brownish colouration or white hairs. *European white:*

Red mackerel tabby European shorthair

eyes may be blue, but these are quite rare and the cat is invariably deaf. Odd-eyed varieties are considered the best sires as they produce kittens with blue eyes, or orange or copper eyes. Not acceptable are pointed muzzles, poor or indefinable eye colour, a yellowing coat or insufficiently boned legs. *European albino:* a blue-eyed solid white cat, which cannot be shown in the ring although it can be registered. The colour of the albino is due to a recessive blue-eyed colour gene; the advantage is that the cat is not deaf. *European cream:* a rarer variety, it should have a faultless cream coat, although streaked or reddish coats appear; a round head, hazel or copper eyes. *European red:* rare; a bright uniform red coat and orange eyes; *European grey:* widespread, popular in Great Britain. Solidly built, with a uniform light-grey coat, copper or orange eyes. *European tabby:* stockily built and highly prized, the European tabby is massive and muscular with broad shoulders. The head is strong, and the cheeks very pronounced. Tabby markings are divided into three patterns; the classic, the mackerel and the patched, as detailed under **American shorthair**, on pages 74–8. *European marbled:* the body is more elongated than that of the tabby, and the cheeks not so pronounced. From the nape of the neck to the tail, the back is crossed by three black bands. On the shoulders,

there are two black blotches in the butterfly shape common to the classic tabby; on the flanks there are two fan-shaped whirls. A wide variety of colours is possible. The European marbled is a famed hunter. *European tortoiseshell:* this is an almost exclusively female variety; any males are sterile. A turtle-shell pattern is made up of well-defined black, red and cream colours, with orange, copper or hazel eyes. *European tortoiseshell and white:* the coat comprises black, red and cream in large well-defined spots, with white areas on the muzzle and chest; orange, copper or amber eyes. *European blue-cream:* a mixture of blue and cream in equal proportions; orange, yellow or copper eyes; another exclusively female breed. *European bi-colour:* black and white, white and blue, orange and white or cream and white, not appearing more than two-thirds white; the ears and mask are coloured.

Origin: probably descending from the African wildcat and introduced throughout the Roman Empire by soldiers as vermin controllers

Personality: rugged, hardy and active, they are quietly spoken, shrewd and untemperamental; self-grooming to a large extent and easy breeders.

Exotic shorthair

Identification: a large to medium cat, Persian in type but with a medium-short dense plush coat

Head: round and massive, with a great breadth of skull. The face is round, the nose short and broad, with a stop. The cheeks are full, as is the well-developed chin.

Eyes: set far apart; large, round and full. They must be blue in the white-haired variety and copper in the black-haired variety; otherwise their colour conforms to the coat colour.

Ears: small, set far apart and low on the head, fitting its rounded contour; round-tipped, tilted forward and not unduly open at the base

Tail: short, in proportion to the body, and carried at an angle lower than the back

Body: a cobby cat, low on the legs and deep in the chest; broad-shouldered. The neck is short and thick, the rump broad and the middle section well-rounded. The back is level, the legs short and strong and quite thick; the forelegs are straight, with large, round firm paws.

Coat: medium in length, being longer than that of other shorthairs; dense, soft in texture and glossy. The coat is springy and does not lie too close to the body.

Colour: the exotic shorthair can be seen in almost every coat colour known; whites (blue eyed, copper-eyed, and odd-eyed), blue, black,

red, cream, chinchilla, shaded silver, shell cameo, shaded cameo, black smoke, blue smoke, cameo smoke; classic and mackerel-patterned tabbies in silver, red, brown, blue, cream and cameo; tortoiseshell, calico, dilute calico, blue-cream and bi-coloured

Origin: the English crossed the British shorthair with the Persian after World War II, to regain the type after their breeding programmes had been disrupted by the war. After setting the type, they bred like to like once again to produce today's British shorthair. In America, the American shorthair breed was secure, but the Persian enjoyed widespread popularity throughout the middle of the twentieth century. Some American shorthair breeders started introducing Persian strains into their stock to produce a more Persian-looking American shorthair. The result was not an American shorthair but the creation of a new breed, somewhere in between the two. In 1966, a hybrid class was formed and called the exotic shorthair.

Personality: generally sweet and gentle, but not always affectionate as some cats tend to be very independent. They enjoy a full family. The coat should be regularly brushed to keep it healthy and soft. Normal litters average four, with the young being born with darker coats than their parents.

128 *Cream tabby*

Havana brown

Identification: a medium-sized cat, elegant and muscular, the standard for which differs slightly from one side of the Atlantic to the other. The British Havana is more Siamese in appearance.

Head: slightly longer than it is wide, with a distinct stop. The head narrows to a rounded muzzle with a slight break behind the brown whiskers. The chin is strong. In the UK, the head forms more of a wedge shape and the face is slightly more rounded but still in the Oriental manner.

Eyes: oval shaped; tending to be more almond-shaped in the UK; green (chartreuse)

Ears: wide-set, large and round-tipped and forward-tilting

Tail: in proportion to the body, medium in length and tapering

Body: medium length and solidly built; not too stocky or too svelte. The legs are also of medium length and the paw pads are pink.

Coat: short, smooth-textured with a lustrous appearance

Colour: in the UK all shades of chestnut brown are accepted, provided that there is no shading, which also applies to the nose and whiskers. In the USA, the colour tends towards a rich warm mahogany brown and the nose leather has a rosy tone.

Origin: although a brown cat was shown in

England as early as 1894 under a breed described as the Swiss mountain cat, the creation of the Havana brown was started in 1950 with a mating between a male chocolate point Siamese and a black shorthair. Offspring of the litter were crossed back to chocolate-gene carrying Siamese, producing a male self-chocolate in 1952. The first Havanas were registered in England in 1954. In America, some Russian blue blood was added and produced a less Siamese-looking cat.

The name was given to the British-bred cat because the coat colour was similar to the colour of tobacco used in the famous Havana cigar. No crossing back to the Siamese is allowed in America as no foreign type is desired, so by breeding Havana brown to Havana brown a different type of cat has been achieved in comparison to the British-bred Siamese-type cat.

Personality: a lively, playful companion, considered to be a one-person cat; they are home-loving and affectionate. Kittens are born with fine fur and their eyes open within the first week.

Japanese bobtail

Identification: a unique breed of Japanese origin, no relation of the tailless Manx cat

Head: long and finely-chiselled, it forms a triangle with gentle curving lines. The cheek bones are high, and there is a noticeable whisker break. The nose is long and well-defined by two parallel lines from tip to brow, with a gentle dip just below eye level. The muzzle is broadish, neither pointed nor blunt and rounds into the whisker break.

Eyes: large, oval with a pronounced slant and must comply with the coat colour

Ears: set wide apart and at right angles to the head, the ears are large and upright

Tail: one of the cat's distinguishing characteristics; the name derives from the short bobtail which should be no more than 12.5cm (5in) long, and is carried upright when the cat is relaxed. The tail bone is usually strong and rigid, jointed only at the base.

Body: well-muscled, long and lean. The legs are long and slender, the hindlegs longer than the forelegs, but when the cat stands the hindlegs are deeply bent so that the back remains level. The front legs and shoulders then form two continuous straight lines close together.

Coat: of medium length, soft and silky with little undercoat. The hair on the tail grows outwards in all directions to create a rabbit-tail or pompom

Tri-coloured Mi-Ke bobtail; note the straight forelegs and bent hindlegs

effect, and disguises the bone structure.

Colour: preferred colours are black, white and red, either as single or double or triple combinations. The division of the colours must be sharp, and white must dominate. Siamese or Abyssinian patterned colours are not acceptable, whereas the tortoiseshell is popular.

Origin: a natural breed originating as a domestic cat, portrayed in Japanese art for centuries. The Japanese Mi-Ke cats are usually tri-coloured and are used symbolically to represent good luck. Imports into the USA in 1908 of bobtailed cats are the first recorded in the West, and the bobtail was first recognised in America in 1971. The bobtail is produced by a single recessive gene. Two bobtail cats will produce all bobtail kittens, even though some may have longer tails than the standard permits.

Personality: they like freedom to roam and explore. Friendly and inquisitive, they are quiet and intelligent, forming strong bonds. They love water and are good swimmers, and also do love to talk in a variety of different tones. They are generally smart and tidy but an occasional light brushing of the coat is advisable. Faults are round or short heads, muscles which are too well-developed and the tail, which must not be too long and must be curved.

136 *Japanese bobtail; this one is actually a red, black and white tricolour*

Korat

Identification: a square cat in profile

Head: heart-shaped, with a slight stop between the nose and forehead. Just above the leather, there is a lion-like downward curve. The jaw and chin are strong and well-developed, not too square or sharply pointed.

Eyes: particularly prominent; big, wide-open and round; luminous green; an amber cast is accepted.

Ears: set high on the head and held erect, the ears are large with a rounded tip and a large flare at the base. Hair inside the ears is sparse.

Tail: medium in length, heavy at the base, tapering to a rounded tip

Body: semi-cobby, with the back carried in a curve. The legs are in proportion to the body, the front legs slightly shorter than the hindlegs, and the paws are oval.

Coat: single-layered; short to medium-length; glossy and fine, lying close to the body

Colour: silver blue, solid and even; the more silver tipping the better. The nose and lips are dark blue or lavender.

Origin: in the Korat province of Thailand. A male and female were imported into America in 1959, were recognised in 1966, and in Europe in 1972.

Personality: intelligent and affectionate, very alert and playful. They are good parents and like the quiet of indoor life.

Malayan

Identification: an American Burmese type

Head: nicely rounded; devoid of any flatness; a full face, with a clearly-defined stop

Eyes: wide set, round, medium-sized; yellow; blue or green eyes are not accepted

Ears: set wide apart; wide at the base, rounded at the tip, and generally in keeping with the face

Tail: of medium length, straight and thick; must not be kinked

Body: medium sized; well-muscled, solid and compact, devoid of any excess fat or flabbiness. The chest is deep and broad, well rounded; the legs are slender.

Coat: short and fine, with a glossy satin finish

Colour: a solid coloured cat with shadings and undertones. The colours are *champagne,* a warm beige; *blue,* medium grey, fawn undertones; and *platinum,* light silver, fawn undertones.

Origin: only recognised in 1980, the breed was created in America and differs from the Burmese only in colour. Not recognised in the UK, where the colours are considered to be Burmese.

Personality: an affectionate, lovable cat; with a loud voice, but dislikes loud noises itself. They do enjoy a large apartment, especially one with a large terrace. Keep the coat clean, preferably with a grooming glove. Females reach their first heat between seven and eight months; the Malayan can be born spontaneously of Burmese parents.

Manx

Identification: a medium-sized, cobby cat; complete with a sack full of legends but no tail

Head: a fairly broad, round head with prominent cheek bones; it has a jowly appearance. Medium in length and in profile it has a definite nose dip; the muzzle is broad and round, the nose long and the chin strong.

Eyes: large, round and full; any colour, provided it is in keeping with the colour of the coat

Ears: triangular, wide at the base, tapering slightly to a point; tilted forwards and turned outwards. Tufting is limited.

Tail: the Manx and Cymric (long-haired Manx) are the only tailless breeds. Apart from detracting from their beauty, the lack of a tail is a handicap as it compromises their balance.

Body: solid, compact; a strong neck and a rounded back, inclined from the shoulders to the haunches. The body is also very deep. At the end of the spine where a tail should begin is a hollow; however, if there is no hollow a rise of the bone at the end of the spine is permitted, provided it does not interrupt the flow of the line of the back. The legs are solid, with the front legs being short and set well apart, showing off the deep chest. The back legs are longer and heavier, with the muscular thighs tapering to a substantial lower leg. The paws are small, neat and well-rounded.

Coat: double coated, with a thick cottony under-

coat and a short, shiny outer coat of good open texture. Quality is more important than colour.

Colour: blue-eyed white, copper-eyed white, odd-eyed white, blue, black, red, cream, chinchilla, shaded silver, black smoke, classic and mackerel tabby in silver, red, brown, blue and cream; tortoiseshell, calico, dilute calico, blue-cream, bi-colour and OMC (other Manx colours). The latter are defined as any other colour or pattern with the exception of those showing hybridisation resulting in the colours chocolate, lavender, the Himalayan pattern, or these combinations with white, and so on. Eye colour is appropriate to the predominant coat colour.

Origin: there are many legends regarding the missing tail of the Manx. One involves Noah and the Ark: when it was ready to leave, the cats had not arrived. Noah was ready to close the doors when they strolled in, quite unconcerned; the gate swung shut on their tails, leaving them tailless and able to produce only tailless kittens.

The Celts, who inhabited the Isle of Man, believed that if you trod on the tail of a cat, a viper (adder) would issue forth and destroy you. A miracle caused tailless cats to be born, and the Celts perpetuated the breed so that they could walk the land without fear.

A shipwrecked galleon of the Spanish Armada deposited tailless cats on the Isle of Man: alterna-

144 *Brown mackerel tabby*

tively, the warriors of the Island cut cats' tails to make plumes for their helmets and so the mother cats learnt to bite off the tails of their kittens and eventually they were born tailless.

The Manx appears to have been a mutation that occurred on the Island which was able to establish itself as a new breed owing to its closed environment. The gene is thought to be an incomplete dominant. If a Manx is out-crossed to other breeds, the taillessness is not altogether lost, but other characteristics are altered. The Manx is not related to the oriental cats such as the Japanese bobtail, nor (as has also been alleged) is it crossed with a rabbit.

On the Isle of Man, the Manx is called a rumpy; they represent good luck and are held in high esteem. Earliest reports of their existence date from 1820, and a Club was founded in 1901. There is a cattery on the Island which provides breeding stock, run by the Douglas Corporation. **Personality:** eager to please and fond of children, the Manx is a gentle cat, often preferring or selecting one member of a family to attach itself to. Quiet and strong, they love to play and are happy in the home; although not adventurers, they are however very adept at tree-climbing. Their coats are soft and so should not be over-brushed, but regular attention is desirable.

Ocicat

Identification: an athletically-built large cat with an attractive spotted coat and a physical resemblance to the Egyptian mau

Head: a modified wedge, well-proportioned; the skull curves slightly from a broad muzzle to the cheeks. The considerable length and squareness of the skull are appropriate.

Eyes: set wide apart; moderately large and angled slightly upward, any colour is acceptable other than blue, with deep colours being preferred

Ears: set at an angle of 45° and standing erect, cornering the top of the head. They are quite large, with tufts vertically aligning the inner sides of the ear cups.

Tail: longish, slim and tapers towards a dark-coloured tip

Body: quite long, deep and full without being bulky. Slightly sprung ribs, and the chest is deep; the back slopes gently upwards towards the rear. The legs are medium to long, and well muscled; the feet are oval.

Coat: short and sleek, it is close-lying and fine-textured

Colour: the distinctive spotted agouti coat pattern of the ocicat is most important. The face is coloured lighter than the rest of the body, the tail tip is the darkest. Colours should be clearly defined on a cream body coat, and are permitted

as follows: silver, chocolate, blue, lavender, cinnamon and fawn (all grouped as silver shades); tawny (brown tabby); chocolate, cinnamon (soft brown); blue, lavender (lilac) and fawn. The tabby pattern is free of blotches, with scattered defined spots being essential; contrast is also extremely important.

Origin: a hybrid breed, the result of crosses between Abyssinians, American shorthairs and a chocolate point Siamese, which has produced a lookalike to the ocelot, a South American wild cat from which it takes its name. The ocicat has now been recognised, although not by all associations, and currently out-crosses are still permitted to the Abyssinian, but these are scheduled to be brought to a stop on 1 January 1995.

Personality: continually busy, the ocicat is a true sportsman and loves the outdoors. They are friendly and have been labelled as attention-getters. They will watch your every move. Ideally suited to a house with a large garden, they require little in the way of brushing or combing and will eat meat, fish, vegetables and rice as a preferred diet. Breeding does not present any problems, but only the finest specimens should be used, both to keep the spots from blotching and because as with any relatively new hybrid, breeders should be cautious.

Oriental shorthair

Identification: self-coloured Siamese type

Head: long; a medium-sized tapering wedge in proportion to the body; no break for the whiskers. The skull is flat; there is no dip or break in the long straight nose; muzzle fine, wedge-shaped, both chin and jaw being medium in size.

Eyes: separated by the width of a single eye, they are almond-shaped and medium in size, slanting towards the nose; normally green; amber, blue and green are permitted, but not odd-eyed white cats.

Ears: large, wide at the base; they continue the lines of the wedge to the tips

Tail: long, thin at the base, tapers to a fine point

Body: tubular, with shoulders and hips of equal width. The abdomen should be tight, the neck long and slender, as are the legs. The hindlegs are longer than the forelegs, paws small and round.

Coat: short and fine-textured; close-lying to the body and glossy; a weekly brushing is enough

Colour: solids, shaded colours, tortoiseshell, smoke and tabby as follows: *white*, even white, eyes blue or green, with yellow accepted, but not odd-eyed; *ebony*, even black, eyes green, yellow accepted; *blue*, light, even grey; *chestnut*, medium-brown including whiskers and nose; *lavender*, even pinkish-grey including the nose and paw pads; *red*, the entire coat should be bright red; *cream*, light cream tending towards

buff, nose and paw pads pink; *silver shaded,* white undercoat with the longer hairs tipped with ebony, chestnut or lavender; the rims around the eyes, nose and lips are lined in black. *Cameo,* white undercoat, with the longer hairs tipped with red; *ebony smoke,* white undercoat, heavily tipped with black; *blue smoke,* white undercoat, heavily tipped with grey; *chestnut smoke,* white undercoat, heavily tipped with brown; *lavender smoke,* white undercoat, heavily tipped with pinkish-grey; *cameo smoke,* white undercoat, heavily tipped with red.

Tabby colours include the spotted and ticked tabby patterns in addition to the more common classic and mackerel patterns. *Spotted tabby pattern:* the spotted markings on the body may vary in size and shape, with evenly-dispersed round spots being preferred. The face mask and forehead should be typically tabby, legs and tail are barred, vest buttons are required on the underside of the belly. The dorsal stripe should be comprised of spots and all spots on the body should be clearly separated. *Ticked tabby pattern:* the body hairs should be ticked with various shades of both the marking colour and the ground colour, and when viewed from above, it should be free from stripes, spots or blotches, with the exception of the dorsal line, which is darker. The underside of the belly may show tabby markings; the face, legs

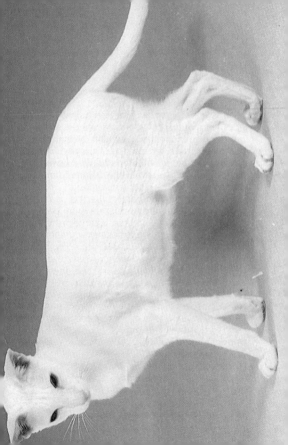

and tail must show tabby markings and there should be a minimum of at least one 'chain' around the neck.

Tabby colours are as follows: *ebony tabby*, coppery brown with black markings; *blue tabby*, bluish-white with dark grey markings; *chestnut tabby*, fawn with brown markings; *lavender tabby*, pale grey with rich pinkish-grey markings; *red tabby*, red with dark red markings; *cream tabby*, pale cream with darker buff-cream markings; *silver tabby*, light silver with black markings; *cameo tabby*, white with red markings.

The other coat colours and patterns for the Oriental shorthair are tortoiseshell, blue-cream, chestnut tortie and lavender-cream. In the USA, the breed includes all Siamese which cannot be registered as either Siamese or colourpoint shorthairs, whereas in the UK, only tabbies, torties and spotted tabbies are considered Oriental shorthairs.

Origin: first appeared as a mutation in the UK, while breeders were trying to perfect the Havana in the 1950s. Development continued more rapidly in America in the 1970s, until the ranks of the Oriental shorthair have reached well over 20 varieties.

Personality: agile and playful, with a softer voice than the Siamese

Russian blue

Identification: a handsome, sweet and thickly-furred blue cat

Head: a wide face with a medium-long straight nose, and a strong chin. The top of the skull is flat and long; the nose leather is slate grey.

Eyes: set wide apart, rounded or oval in shape and must always be green, ranging from light emerald green to dark bottle green

Ears: set far apart towards the side of the head, the ears are longish, wide at the base with the tips more pointed than rounded. The skin on the ears is thin, with very little inside furnishing and little hair on the outside.

Tail: a long, straight, smooth and tapering tail, with quite a thick base

Body: fine-boned, long and graceful; the legs are also long and fine-boned with small paws, slightly rounded lavender pink or mauve pads. The neck is long and slender but appears short under the thick coat and because of the high placement of the cat's shoulder blades.

Coat: double-coated, and standing out from the body. The fur is short and dense, comprised of fine hairs giving a plush and lustrous finish.

Colour: a clear, even, bright blue throughout, with no trace of white. However, shade varies, with lighter or lavender shades being preferred in America, and in the UK a more medium blue.

Origin: at the end of the nineteenth century, cats

which were believed to have originated in Arch-
angel in Russia appeared, with a silvery-blue
short dense plush coat. These wild cats were trap-
ped in northern Russia for their fur, which was
both beautiful and thick. The double coat served
to protect them against the severe climate of the
near-Arctic.

The Vikings may have taken these cats to
Sweden and then into England, where the first
Russian blue was shown in 1880 and they were
judged along with all of the other shorthaired
blues. In 1912 the class was split into British blue
and foreign blues, with the Russian blues in the
latter category. The name was not separately
registered until 1939; it is a natural breed, its
colour, type and coat all being unique. The best
Russian blues now come from Sweden. There are
small differences between the English and American standards, with higher ear settings required in
England and the English type being slightly more
'foreign' than the American.

Personality: quiet, softly-spoken individuals,
gentle and shy; extremely affectionate with each
other, they make excellent parents. Normal litters
are four, and only purebred Russian blues should
be used in order to avoid deterioration of the line.
Grooming is minimal and should not be over-
done; the coat should not be flattened.

Scottish fold

Identification: a cobby, powerful cat with a pleasant expression and folded-down ears

Head: massive and round, with full rounded cheeks and well-developed chin, a broad jaw, and a rather large nose. The whisker pads are well rounded

Eyes: large, round and full; well opened; the eye colour is related to the coat colour

Ears: set wide apart and distinguished by a definite fold line, which can vary from a small tightly-folded ear to a larger, looser folded ear. However, the ear is generally small, folded forward and down at the top to the ear pocket. Kittens may have only a slight fold.

Tail: can be either short with a rounded tip, or longer and tapering slightly; in either case, the tail is thick at the base and not too flexible

Body: short, broad across the shoulders and rump; the cat is compact and well-balanced, with a full broad chest. The neck is short and thick, the legs of medium length and the toes well rounded.

Coat: thick and dense, soft in texture and elastic

Colour: basically the same as the American shorthair; blue, red, white, black, cream, chinchillas, shadeds, torties, smokes, tabbies, patches and bi-coloured. The tabby colours can be divided into three patterns; the classic, which has been more fully described on pages 74–8, and has broad, clearly-defined dense markings; the

mackerel pattern of thinner light and dark bands, and patched, which is brown, silver or blue, with patches of red and/or cream.

Origin: the first Scottish fold appeared as a mutant in a litter on a farm in Perthshire, Scotland. The cat had a pure white coat, short thick tail and ears that folded down onto the head. This cat was bred to a red tabby, and the resultant litter contained one male fold. A second litter born to the original fold and a British shorthair produced a litter of five Scottish folds. These became the base stock of the new breed. It was recognised in America in 1974, and in England in 1977. The best breeding results from crosses with either British shorthairs or American shorthairs, and produces litters which are basically 50 per cent Scottish folds; however, it is important that the quality of the erect-eared cats used for breeding is excellent, so as to guard against loss of type. Only at four weeks of age can it be established whether the kittens will have folded or straight ears.

Personality: friendly, gentle and sweet, these home-loving cats are wonderful companions, good with strangers and children alike. Good hunters, they love the outdoors but are equally content to live indoors. A hardy breed, they need little grooming or attention.

164 *A female calico Scottish fold*

Siamese

Identification: a most elegant cat, with a body devoid of any fat, eyes that are always a deep vivid blue, and the colourpoint coat pattern

Head: a long, tapering wedge-shaped head, medium in size, with no break for the whiskers. The skull is flat and there is no dip in the nose or bulges in the face. The nose is long and straight with no break; the muzzle is fine and also wedge-shaped, the chin and jaw medium in size.

Eyes: almond-shaped, medium-sized, no less than the width of a single eye apart; slanting towards the nose, echoing the lines of the wedge

Ears: continuing the wedge, the ears are wide at the base, large and pointed; set well apart

Tail: long, thin and tapering to a point

Body: medium in size, long and svelte; fine bones and trim muscles. Shoulders and hips are the same width; the abdomen is tight, neck and legs long and slender; hindlegs higher than the front; paws are refined, small and oval

Coat: short and fine-textured, lying close to the body and with a glossy appearance

Colour: the coat of the Siamese is pointed, and recognised in the USA only in seal point, chocolate point, blue point and lilac point; the eight additional colours recognised in the UK are tabby point, tortie tabby point, red point, seal tortie point, blue tortie point, chocolate tortie point, lilac tortie point and cream point. These are

recognised in America as colourpoint shorthairs. Self-coloured Siamese are recognised as Oriental shorthairs in the USA, and foreign shorthairs in the UK, but whereas all Oriental shorthairs are self-coloured Siamese, not all foreign shorthairs are self-Siamese.

The points are the face mask, ears, legs, feet and tail, and have to be a rich dark colour in contrast to the rest of the body. The mask must visibly join the eyes, with tracings to the ears, covering the entire face including the whisker pads but not the top of the head. *Seal point:* the most common, and the original Siamese colour. The adult cat is beige, light fawn on the back and shading to almost-white on the underbelly and chest. The mask, ears, nose leather, legs and tail are a sharply defined and definite seal brown; gloves are pure white, the paw pads pink. *Chocolate point:* ivory, with no shading. The points, except for white gloves, are a warm milk chocolate; nose leather is cinnamon pink and paw pads pink. *Blue point:* bluish white for a cold appearance, shading almost to white on the stomach and chest. The points are deep blue, the gloves pure white; nose leather slate colour, paw pads pink; the deeper blue and more violet in tone the eyes, the better. *Lilac point:* a cold, glacial almost-white without shading. Points are a pinkish frosty-grey; the gloves are pure white, nose leather lavender pink,

paw pads pink.

Origin: the Siamese lived in the Royal Palace, guarding both it and the Buddhist temples. These royal cats were kept quite separate and were carefully bred, unlike the town cats that roamed freely, reproducing their crossed eyes, improper markings or kinked tails.

The royal cats were not sold, but occasionally one would be given; the first purebred Siamese temple cat arrived in England in 1884 as a gift from the King of Siam to the British Consul-General, Mr Owen Gould. The standard was drawn up in 1902, at which time all Siamese were to be seal points. The first Siamese in America had arrived in a similar way in 1878, as a gift to First Lady Mrs Rutherford B Hayes.

Personality: sensitive, complex and very moody from one day to the next, Siamese are lively and lovable, alert and playful, with a temperament all their own. They live willingly indoors but will run amok, jumping and clawing to burn up their energy. Brush daily with a medium-hard brush.

Singapura

Identification: small and muscular

Head: round, with a short blunt nose. The muzzle is broad, the chin strong; there is a definite whisker break and a stop. The nose leather is pale to dark salmon.

Eyes: large, almondish in shape, showing a slight slant, and very open

Ears: set at a medium distance apart; large, wide at the base and slightly pointed at the tip

Tail: medium to long, straight without kinks, slender but not too thin, and round at the tip

Body: equal body length and shoulder height; the muscles are sound, the legs heavily boned and strong; the feet are small and oval

Coat: very short and fine in texture, close-lying and with a silky appearance

Colour: existing breeders have limited colours to an ivory ground colour ticked with dark brown, and a bi-colour of white and ticked tabby

Origin: a very old breed, native to Singapore, where it is to be found free-roaming and in a wide variety of colours. Not popular in its home country; the first imports to America were in the mid-1970s, and it is still very rare there.

Personality: fearless and inquisitive, these street cats are used to the noisy bustle of life but tend to be quiet themselves and very adaptable. They require little attention other than a moderate brushing.

Snowshoe

Identification: a recent man-made breed, for which no standard has yet been set, so there may be variations in reported descriptions

Head: broad and round, with full cheeks; the muzzle is also rounded, the chin strong and well-developed. There is a stop in the nose line.

Eyes: large and round, with the outer corner just hinting at an upward tilt; turquoise or rich teal

Ears: set well apart, broad at the base, medium in length and rounded at the tips

Tail: medium in length; well-proportioned, not too thin and rounded at the tip

Body: long, well-developed body with thick-set medium-length legs; large, round, firm paws

Coat: soft, short and glossy; not too fine

Colour: seal point (fawn coat with dark brown points) or blue point (bluish-white coat with dark grey points). White markings on the feet may reach to the ankle on the front legs and the hock on the hindlegs; a white chin is acceptable.

Origin: a hybrid created by crossing a Siamese with a bi-coloured American shorthair. The first generation does not have colourpoints, so must be crossed back to another hybrid to arrive at the snowshoe. Variation is slowly being confined, and a definite standard may be reached soon.

Personality: so far, the snowshoe is showing inquisitiveness and affection, tending to be easy-going; they make excellent companions

Sphynx

Identification: a hard, muscular cat with a medium bone structure; the sphynx has a high blood temperature and also has the ability to sweat

Head: on the small side, not too triangular, slightly longer than it is wide, with a definite whisker break; a stop to the bridge of the nose, with another above the eyes. The sphynx has no whiskers or eyebrows. The cheeks are flat, the chin small and strong.

Eyes: oval in shape, the colour is in keeping with the coat colour except where green, gold or hazel eye colour is acceptable in the black and white parti-colours. The eyes incline outwards.

Ears: large and wide, quite triangular and rounded at the tips

Tail: long, tapering from the base to the tip; it should be in proportion to the body

Body: medium in length, with a modified 'tuck' behind the ribs. A barrel chest gives a broad appearance to the legs, and the neck is long and slender; the legs are of medium length, the paws oval with long slender toes.

Coat: very short down, almost invisible to sight and touch, with tight-packed soft hair on the points (ears, muzzle, tail, and feet). A line of short wiry hair running down the spine is allowable; the coat of the sphynx feels like suède.

Colour: includes solid white, black, blue, red

and cream; chinchilla, shaded silver, shell cameo (red chinchilla), shaded cameo (red shaded); smokes including black smoke, blue smoke, and cameo smoke; classic tabby in standard colours with the characteristic 'M' marking on the forehead, banded legs and tail, butterfly markings on the back of the head and shoulders, necklaces, vertical lines running down the length of the back and solid blotches on the sides. Mackerel tabby and patched tabby patterns in brown, blue and silver, tortoiseshell, calico, dilute calico and bi-coloured are also accepted.

Origin: a spontaneous mutation that appeared in Canada in 1966 to a black and white domestic shorthair. For out-crosses, the domestic shorthair is used because it was one of the original parents. As in the rex, the mutation changed the type in addition to the coat.

Personality: these are very sociable cats, but not fond of being handled, although they won't mind walking over you. They will seek out a warm place to sit on, and will sit with both hindlegs under the hocks together, backside in the air. Being hairless, the sphynx does not need brushing but does need special skin care to give protection against the elements. It is also important that they should not receive mouse nips, and that they should live indoors and in a temperate climate as they are susceptible to serious colds.

178 *Red and white sphynx*

Tonkinese

Identification: a Burmese and Siamese mix

Head: moderately triangular, with more length than width; the skull forms a modified wedge. There is a noticeable stop in the nose; the cheeks are not prominent and the muzzle is blunt, with a slight whisker break.

Eyes: almond-shaped, slightly rounded at the bottom, set wide apart; blue-green in colour

Ears: medium-sized; broad at the base, oval-tipped and pricked froward

Tail: long and tapering, proportionate to the body; wider at the base than the tip

Body: medium-sized, beautifully proportioned, with long, slim legs; the hindlegs are slightly higher than the front legs, the paws oval and small

Coat: silky to touch, lustrous to look at, the coat is close-lying and medium-short in length

Colour: basically Siamese coat colours, but with names unique to the Tonkinese: *natural mink,* a rich warm brown, points a dark chocolate brown to sable; nose leather dark brown. *Honey mink,* a warm ruddy brown with a reddish cast; points a rich chocolate brown, nose leather a medium dark brown. *Champagne mink,* a soft warm beige; as the cat matures, so the coat gradually darkens. The points are a warm light brown, the nose leather may be either pink or cinnamon. *Blue mink* can vary from a soft blue-

grey to medium blue-grey; points are a medium blue to slate, nose leather is blue-grey. *Platinum mink*, a light silver-grey; points are pewter-grey.

Dense colour is required on the mask, ears, feet and tail, and the points must harmonise with the ground colour.

Origin: the result of crossing Siamese with Burmese, possibly enhancing the best characteristics of both, the Tonkinese is recognised in North America but not yet in Great Britain. The coat colour is determined by the point colour of the Siamese used. Commonly the first generation of Tonkinese is produced using a seal-point Siamese bred to a sable Burmese, and produces a 100 per cent Tonkinese. Tonkinese are only bred to Tonkinese, and not back to their parents.

Personality: friendly and outgoing, the Tonkinese is affectionate and a beautiful show cat. They are curious and active and exceptionally good-natured. They enjoy exercise and are best suited to a garden environment. Regular brushings are required and the occasional bath keeps the coat in show condition. Litters often produce kittens with white or off-white coats, and occasionally solid-coloured coats, and although these cannot be shown, nonetheless they may be perfect in all other respects.

The Tonkinese combines the best of the Siamese and Burmese

Glossary

abscess: a painful swelling containing pus that may occur on any part of the cat's body, and is often accompanied by a fever, a reaction to infection; most commonly caused by wounds inflicted during fights.

acne: a skin disease affecting the area of the lips and chin. It is usually the result of an incorrect diet, constipation or hormonal dysfunctions.

ageing: basically a cat is old when it reaches nine years of age. It is advisable to adjust their diet by reducing the amount of meat and increasing the amount of fish, fresh cheese and broth.

alopecia: a pathological skin condition, resulting in the loss of hair, with the fur falling out in patches; the cat should be treated by a vet.

arthritis: a painful inflammation of the joints, normally caused by the ageing process, but also attributable to excessive dampness over a period of time. A veterinary clinic will be able to provide remedies for the pain; do not use those intended for humans.

ascarids: round worms. Small, cylindrical parasites 2.5-10cm (1-4in) in length, they are pinkish in colour and live in the intestines of cats. They are easiest to detect in the faeces. The larvae can be transmitted from a nursing mother cat to her kittens, and therefore it is wise to have kittens wormed within the first four weeks of being born. Obtain medicine from the vet and disinfect the cat's environment to destroy all eggs.

asthma: symptoms are laboured breathing, chest constriction and coughing. The cat will require plenty of rest in a dry place, and possibly adjustment to diet, on which the vet will advise.

breed: a variety of a species, among which aesthetic and psychological qualities are passed on from one generation to the next in a highly-selective manner

burns: usually caused by boiling water or heated objects; most easily overlooked as no welts appear on the cat's skin and the fur is not disturbed. Check by seeing if the hair pulls out easily from the affected area; if so, then the burn is serious and needs immediate treatment. Apply ice or cold compresses to the burn in the interim.

cat registration: the genealogical listing of all purebred cats, with their detailed pedigrees. A record of all members' animals is kept by the relevant cat fancy association to which they belong. A cat must be recorded in the files before a pedigree can be issued.

cattery: where breeders mate cats, always with the aim of maintaining the purity of the breed, and of supplying kittens for sale

clubs: responsible for the organisation of breeders, exhibitions, judges, owners and the continual checking of standards of a specific breed

deafness: hearing may be affected by the

hardening of the duct, accumulation of wax, perforation of the eardrum, or catarrh and all of these may lead eventually to deafness

diabetes: mainly caused by a faulty diet, and affecting older cats. The cat loses weight, drinks much more water, urinates frequently and becomes progressively weaker. Urine samples are needed for diagnosis and treatment is by insulin and diet control.

dysentery: a lower-intestine infection, giving rise to fever, pain and diarrhoea, which may be severe. Faulty diet, colds, feline enteritis, intestinal parasites or poisoning are all possible causes, and the cat should be kept indoors in the warmth without food until a vet can be called.

eczema: a skin inflammation which causes reddening, the formation of vesicles and often scabs, aggravated by the cat's scratching to relieve the discomfort. May be caused by faulty liver function, vitamin deficiency, allergies, poor skin care or food poisoning. The diet must include fish, fresh cheese, buttermilk or yoghourt, and injections are available at the veterinary clinic to prevent liver damage as well as topical lotions to ease the itching.

exercise: an absolute necessity for almost all breeds; those which do not have access to a garden must be encouraged to play indoors

feline infectious enteritis or panleuco-

penia: a viral disease, often fatal if not immediately treated in young cats or kittens; all kittens should be vaccinated at about ten weeks against it. The symptoms are listlessness, loss of appetite, extraordinary thirst, a rapid rise in temperature and loss of condition, and also vomiting; if a kitten is vomiting and looks ill, the veterinary surgeon should be called immediately.

feline respiratory diseases: upper respiratory infections (URI) include rhinotracheitis (FVR), calicivirus (FC1), feline pneumonitis (FPN), feline reovirus infection (FRI) and *felinae syncytia*-forming viruses (FSV), all of which have similar symptoms and should be vaccinated against in kittens.

fever: a cat's temperature should range between 100.5-102.5°F; if it rises further, and the cat has little appetite, is listless and unsociable, it needs swift diagnosis.

heatstroke: very young kittens and old or overweight cats are particularly vulnerable. The symptoms are high temperature, staggering, and collapse, possibly accompanied by vomiting, and the cat should be moved immediately to a cool place and cold compresses should be applied, and circulation improved with body massage.

heredity: the transmission of characteristics, both physical and psychological, from one generation to the next. Traits may be inherited from distant ancestors as well as the immediate parents, or in part from one parent and in part from the other.

hydrophobia or rabies: a disease which may affect dogs, wolves, cats, rodents and humans, usually transmitted in the bite of a diseased animal. Symptoms include seeking the dark, irritability, scratching, trying to hide and being unable to drink because of paralysis of the glottis. Vaccine is available for cats.

insect stings or bites: become noticeable when they swell up; if the sting has been left in, remove it with tweezers, but if one is not visible and the swelling continues, seek veterinary help

mastitis: acute inflammation of the nipples in a nursing cat, as a result of infection or a blockage in the mammary glands, or sometimes a wound.

oestrus: ovulation in the female cat; being 'in heat'

otitis: inflammation of the outer ear, often preventable by regular cleansing of the ear to discourage eczema, mange mites or dirt.

parasites: fleas, ticks, and lice may live on the cat's fur or skin, and can be eliminated by using pesticide-impregnated collars or powders or some compresses. Internal parasites in the cat's stomach, intestine or blood may include roundworm, hookworm, heartworm, protozoans, strongyloides and tapeworms. Left untreated, all of these will leave the animal in a weakened condition and therefore more vulnerable to disease.

respiratory ailments: often the first symptoms are sneezing, watering of the eyes, listlessness and loss of appetite. An increased breathing rate or fever should prompt veterinary help. See also **feline respiratory diseases**.

ringworm: a highly-contagious skin disease caused by a fungus; always wear gloves when handling a cat suspected of having ringworm, as it can be transmitted to humans. It appears in patches, often growing out from the centre in a circular pattern, and veterinary treatment is a must.

shedding: many animals, including cats, replace their coats at the start of the warm summer weather; daily brushing is particularly important during this moult. Excessive loss of hair or bare patches may indicate the onset of eczema, dermatitis or a parasitic infection.

standard: describes height and length, coat colour and pattern, consistency of fur, eye colour, shape of head and muzzle and the character of the breed, as required by the cat fancier's association.

tail: the shape, length and thickness of the tail are important aspects of its appearance, and are described in the standard for the breed. More prosaically, it is used as an instrument of balance, and is a helpful indicator of mood in the different ways the cat will move it.

tumour: abnormal tissue growth, especially frequent in old cats. Benign tumours can be removed by surgery and will not return, but malignant ones may recur elsewhere, even after the original tumour has been removed.

ulcer: must be treated by the veterinary surgeon; it is caused by gastroenteritis, stomatitis, parasites or having eaten or drunk something corrosive. The symptoms are loss of appetite, vomiting, diarrhoea, depression or nervousness, and expression of pain.

urination: territorial spraying is characteristic of some male cats, but both male and female may spray on a wall and if this continues it may be a sign of trouble in the urinary system. Tiny stones may obstruct the urinary canal, resulting in the retention of toxic wastes which may cause irreversible kidney damage, and it is best to seek treatment immediately.

vaccination: all kittens, at an age recommended by the veterinary surgeon, should be vaccinated against several upper respiratory diseases, feline infectious enteritis (panleukopenia) and rabies.

water: should always be available to a cat, as although in the wild they drink only once a day, a total lack of water soon results in dehydration. In cases of stomach ailments, it should be limited in quantity.

Index